My
Zorba

My Zorba

Danielle Pafunda

BLOOF BOOKS

Published by Bloof Books
www.bloofbooks.com
Central New Jersey

Bloof Books are distributed to the trade via Ingram and other wholesalers
in the US, Bertrams and Gardners in the UK, or directly from the press.
Individuals may purchase them from our website, from online retailers
such as Powells.com and Amazon.com, or request them from their favorite
bookstores. (Please support your local independent bookseller whenever
possible.)

ISBN: 978-0-6151-9593-3

For you, you pet, you bête noire,
you tender and gentle beast.

"If you become a fish in a trout stream," said his mother,
"I will become a fisherman and I will fish for you."

—Margaret Wise Brown, *The Runaway Bunny*

My Sea Legs

From then on, Zorba called me "Princess of Quite-a-Lot."
She said my body became a praise-shack. From the catalogue,
a new bed. From the neighbor's bed, a lace wig. She stenciled
the ripe pets herself. She upholstered my vanity table in shag.

She took aside her little nephew and for fun they mapped a city.
In the pocket, she had charcoals, pastels, crayons, ochres. Rot.
He drew a drawbridge, she drew a gangplank. He an awning,
she an armory. In the city hall, a buck hung. Black lung.
Gallows. They drew a dock for me, a to and fro for bad days,
and wrought a trip-trap iron caisson with the top down.

What Historicity

Or, Zorba, let me do what I want. That Zorba told me,
when I was a little girl, don't stand like that. Don't cock
(blasé!) your hip like that, don't limp your wrist, your
tip, your chew.

She said.

Zorba, get onto my back. Repeat. In the peek-a closet,
in the creature's peek. Under the stairs. A tabula rasa.
A break in the spindle results in a headspace. A margarine tub.

Where we hung the ovary of homestead.

Née Providential

My little mommydaddy, my little broken rib. My little sterile

        (strip. You had a sister with a wig that looked like you.
        A transistor. You made a sister look like you. You had
        a little pocket watch.)

A hired house to haunt me. I had a house ghost. You hired.

I searched your suitcase for a jewel you sewed. I searched for tickets, penmanship, sick tags, permanent. A whiff of home. We stitched your picture in my lining.

A Quarter-Hour of Recess

In the schoolyard, Zorba wanted to compare genies.
With another girl. A panty-waist. He called me Russian.
The Russians are coming. A broken strand of panties.
Wind. Then, profile, he coaxed a match from the placket.

A set of stumps at various heights, rendered the red, blue,
yellow absolute. We ventured an alligator, a predation,
irked by little feet as the troll was. Irked by gruff not gruff
enough. The permanent shiver. We rode it.

He took turns on me. We performed a dance known as
"under doggies," and when that was banned, we called it
"under over." In the present tense, the school demanded.
I, you, we, they forgive. He and she forgives.

When I tried to cover the hair with pancake, Zorba
intercepted. She patted down the razor blade. The laugh.
Later, Zorba, her own blade in hand. Her brittle.

She put pantyhose over her athletic shorts. And a skirt
over that. I did the same. A porcelain crematorium
over my house. And invited her for tea. For symptomatic.

(Even now, on the thirtieth, I have a little down. I have
a facial bleeder.)

Tribune

At the tractor pull, Zorba asked me to read their cards.
Her sergeant at arms an affluent heir, her friend county
sheriff a closeted phobe. She asked for a profit margin.
Particulate. And although her brother still lost at sea,
I would not read the card for frontage.

I would not read the card for Christmas. The card for a prig
in a cage, thus fishnet. Hoaxed by a priest. Nor bind

her breasts with bandages, iodine. The demolition derby,
a windowless visage. Widowless. The gas tank removed,
repaired, replaced with a pig's heart. A paw on the bible.

I pawed at the bible, a personal entry. The footnote. Taffy.
Behind the concrete ribcage, beneath the opaline bleacher,
I removed my zipper from its package. I buried my zipper.

Zorba regarded the gluttonous [moon]. She had
acquired a [gossamer] hickey and pasted it to her
[nape], her treacle handy [bosom]. She devoured
a [nightbird] and chucked its bones from the [precipice].
The [chasm]. The [cliff's edge], the pallid [flower]
of [solitude] spanked, she [gazed] piqued at the [waves]
[cavorted]. Not little, the [corpse] [sung] [wept] [holy],
Zorba could have [swooned] but the pills were rather
less than [ten]. Or the what-ought rather less than [loaded].

Rallying on the Plank, the Porch Swing Leans In

The honeysuckle weeps like a lesion. Zorba in her cups
hands me a sickle feather. She tells me to rid the rooster of his
punch. His prim. In the extended shimmy of a late spring dusk
I see outlined clearly the rogue hair in Zorba's narrow chin.

She gestures with the coke bottle. To the bottle. She angles
the glass against my skirt. Scleroid. The curtain notches down.

With Zorba's fingers, I have seen the shape of the triangle.
The shape of the hole and the shape of the plaintiff. I have
encountered the shape of a blade of grass, which slips just
between the two doors of the porch. Screen and otherwise.

Zorba might argue that, for the third time in a year, I had
become hysterically pregnant. Indeed, might I. Here
is my handle, and spout. Lay off it, might she, and might I
take my belly out from under the coverall. The crawl.

Later, she would return from the market with an extension cord.
For hanging the chandelier. In a bucket out to sea, she might.
Hum. In a brisket, in as much. All the while in an afghan,
knitting my own tether, lashing one plum to the next, the next
to a wad from a sheaf.

It was, in the interim, a very happy Christmas.

Building a Nest, the A–Z

I was so jacked up on vitamins, I proceeded straight through
the caution door. Permeated. The metal bar and the alarm
signature. Zorba had made me a wig of chocolate and stray.
He had applied a kohl liner to my various tendons and various
points of pressure.

The subtleties of the courtyard lit up one by one, drowning out
the pinkish grotto in its every corner.

I was so KO'd, so tanked, so regal, furtive, dormant, a champ.
I was so full of vitamin mash and protein.

Zorba would later find the stain on the egg wool carpet,
behind the grandfather clock. He would be righting the dust
and distributing the bleach. His proper scrub brush narrow
at the head and ergonomic in the hand.

Go Starboard, Go Further, a Flare

On the SS Zorba, we lodge in the HanselandGretel suite. Stateroom.
We lodge our belongings in the toehold, and what togs remain we
graduate into. We dinner. We deck with the captain, a stroll in the
balloon light. We deck the captain, the gunner comes running.

Snail the passage so that in the phosphorescence of shipwreck,
I will be able to find you.

Waste no time in this.

Zorba waltzed the instructor's, the inspector's daughter. The loveliness

of his mouth surprised

me. Over the hilt of an ice cream

cone. He had a hand for the small of my back. In public,

a working holiday. A hold over. He had a pair

of character

shoes. In the beginning,

I could receive, but could not contain,

and this

was the source of a nettle.

A bet between the ship's captain and starboard.

I watched

the entire scene in my compact.

A Parsimonious Holiday

At the Mexican restaurant, Zorba wanted the kitten. A scar
I got, a parsing. Zorba wanted the leather stitching from
the waitress's apron. A task. A golden egg, a species feather.
The mango in the harlot's locket, or so he called it, running
his finger around the ridge. The fool-cramp.

The tooth of a jimmied lock. I crossed the carpet, and smoothed
its tussled furs. In the closet. A determined gray stiletto.
The hangers were hooked to the bar, the rungs to the pants
by a series of pins through which one could look, could squint.
Safely. A series of animals. A turgescent processional.

But they had already gathered us in the amphitheater, for a live
performance of the 911 call. They said, "great reviews." Said,
"present company excluded," while Zorba referred to his program.

Zorba read from the glossary, *it is a wind instrument made from a piece of wood which has only one aperture where it can be blonn at. However, long time ago, stone was used and later on when goats and sheeps raising were introduced theirs bones, especially the tibia, for this sonorous instruments making were used as well.*

It would be interesting to see what happened next.

Were the Drawing Room a Portion

Zorba had invited her pals the apostles. To welcome home.
The one with the quill in his back, the one with the lamp
in his throat. A pectoral. Dance. The one with the mail.
Drove the boat, waded ashore. With the ladies, dance.
In the rosy beam of venetian bone.

On the sofa, Zorba fastens her forearm to the armrest.
Ties her tooth to a can. She screams for the ouija board,
a game of charades. Plutonic. For the cribbage board,
a peg tucked under each nail.

Later, an apostle would handle me ought in the yard.
By my nape, he would march me in a tight. The tempo
larval, the crescendo elective.

Zorba's little nephew was *roller-coaster-scaried*. Zorba's neph examined his *pubity*. His *s-perm* had begun to be *manfutured*. A red-hair nicked the glass from a narrow in the entryway. To wait him on his bed. He slept.

He whispered to Zorba. Some types will release fluid. With a dog whistle aimed at my *innie,* he said, *her's inflated.*

For the first time in years, I felt my tentacle flex,
curl and uncurl in he loves me, loves me not fashion,
in party favor timbre, in a mile of shoreline friction.
That slick green tube, that horn of plenty.

In the vestibule once were wellies, were Welsh poppies
and Weltschmertz. In the vestibule of that Wendy house,
that matched its swatches to Zorba's lesser looms.
The household were all clothespins and on each finger,
each furled. Each yarn hair, and the smudge mouth.

And soon thereafter I stiffened.

A Second Opinion Is Sought

In earnest, the quack examined me. In his physician's parlor,
and Zorba came for the up and up. The tigerskin rug. A lazy
sheet revealed a cream-laden upholstery. A crescent shape.
The quack gave me a position, in which I got on the slab.

Zorba had his penis by the throat. The count was in. The numberer.
He had a vase of predicates. Zorba slipped these into her pocket.
She took a tongue depressor when he turned his back. To read me.
To angle my knee into my chest. A stork in relief. Zorba agreed.

And then the quack was singing. His lip was wet with woe betide.
Zorba took her breast out of its sling. She offered me the room key.
She offered me a trade. And he said to wait five months. And
we all agreed. The register of good health stamped our hands.
Our waterlogged and vacant tempers.

(A Transportation Ballad

He pointed my foot to my mouth, a dramatic reenactment.
With the town's tenderheart, I had flounced. Tartly.
The militarized zone. A beachhead rendered my stomach
a money pit. Phobic gauze held my headwound in place.
My self-inflicted. Still, my walking papers hadn't come,
and I went to the porch with a visor. With an egregious telescope.

He pointed, Zorba. His long finger a shimmer, a heatstroke.
He explained America like this: a weapon in the bushes. Like
this: you live here. Like this, you wait for a bus, you step on
through a pneumatic door, you wheeze a yellow protein, ring
your neck with black plumes of exhaust. Or rather, you wait
for the fire truck to smote you.)

I make a garish bouquet.

Wallowing in a Science, the Cupboard Bares All

She eyed the suture in my butter dish. I'd put all the evidence
of uncanny double in the refrigerator. Including the folic acid
and the cod liver oil. To preserve them, in case of inquiry.

The analyst considered a cottage cheese container. Zorba
had never been to that particular prison, but she claimed
to have once shared a cell with a cyst. She got on the horn
toot sweet to tell her pals what had gone down. Vicarious.

Victorious.

In the pseudo-unmediatedness, unmitigatedness. In the simulacrum
of predawn, I wore the camouflage of red terry cloth and performed
tracheotomies on the sugar ants, until each could breathe
through the thorax, uninterrupted by guilt.

In the Museum of Your Two Halves

In the museum of your two halves, I find my lost car key.
On the East coast, Easter has rolled over into snowstorm.
The sputter of my brake lights. I take you by the handbrake.
Fold your legs around my cup and saucer. Fold your
good eye around my packet of petition letters to the dean.

Zorba waits for me, off exit twenty-six. He carries a battle
axe and a carburetor. Or a different decade. He carries flint
for the lighter and a jar of red granules like those which sugar.
A petal cookie. He warned me the wool blanket. He

Ahem. Zorba. You'd better look at this. Your clorox
has come full circle. I parse defeat. I halo painstakingly
for shore.

I could only think in small pieces!
I could not speak in first person! The copper wire
strung!
From my armpit, a personality exam, a pelvic
diatribe.

Long distance, Zorba attempted a natural selection. He spoke
in tubal sequence. Sequins. His halter made the line buzz.
The fabulist fixed the plumbing, and fixed 'er good.

But wasn't your marathon, Zorba? Wasn't your soap
in the sock, the sock itself, bound off at the cuff? Or knot
itself, the soap a beat behind?

Zorba called me from Pittsburgh, where he was learning
to diagnose by numbers. He wanted to send me a picture
from space, a pronounced physiological term. He'd been
to the factory, and there a dumb son wore a pretty segment.
A machine-like wing to wind him up.

He could not recall an experience of gulch.

The Cold Sack, an Envelope

Breathe easy, Zorba. The hair. My strand is black.
They will send you my blood in a vial. Two vials,
with the narrow lavender stopper, the thicker flesh
colored stopper. In a mannequin's vein.

They will send you my carcinogen glove,
wrapped in a cadaver. In actuality, wrapped
like a fish, head first. You will apply an adhesive
to a strip of fabric from an embroidered bodice.
In a practical box. A pair of pinking shears.

Whether the scented notepaper. Whether the wax
seal, the itemized invoice, the stamp, which will feature
the Kennedy children. Whether the stopper will.

Fondly, Yours, Sincerely, My Love

Dear Grandmother. Zorba is at it again. She's fat as a sow.

I threw her into the basement, I diapered her, and now she's
nosing around the sump pump. I feed her through an eye-
dropper. I feed directly into her neck. I've changed her
prescription. Into each of seven blue surgeon's cups,
I count twenty-two pills.

(An iron pill. It is spring green and slips like a slim pen from
Grandfather's apoplectic fingers. An Esther-C in 1000 units.
Tang like the rent skin of the gums that precedes eating one's
own heart out. An E capsule. A taut oval of oil, a dreamery
of viscous remains. A Co-Q10, burnt sienna, a B-Complex
with a soft scorpion center. Malic Acid. Selenium. The Zinc
that makes her squirm.)

And I leave them. On the edge of the laundry sink. A hose
for the swallowing, a net to catch the cartilage.

In the Iron Caisson

Dear Aunt Hemorrhage, Dear Uncle Rottweiler,

The f-up was the industrial red dye. The connection was bogus.
In the morning, I glued your robin's nest to the sill. Zorba ratchets like
    a turnstile.
In the cedar closet, he discovered the microscope. A corrugation.
I secured in an earring the grain of salt. The pencil shaving.
Meant for a ticket. Meant for a placard. Meant for a vial of progesterone.

Dear Martin Grainger,

I will only wear the speculums for so long. In the basement,
Zorba completes his psychogeographical survey. He reminds me
of the time he locked himself in with the Demerol. Of the time
he dismantled the knob on the bathroom door. Scissor.
When I eagled the orange. Kitchen carpet. Permit me.
I siphon a vowel with which to respond.

Dear Argyle Our Frosty Morning,

The laundry's overdone. Zorba cites bleach, cites propane tank. I've
rerouted the exhaust pipe. From the dryer. Against the limestone,
the forecast bleeds. From the inside, I pack the belly. Zorba checks.
Check-minuses. Here the fairy's ring, the collar striated, compromised.

He circles in lipstick the lipstick-print lips. In lipstick the grease,
which angles like a tumor and renders a window where once
was a badge. Puppet. Read the bottle and it says faction.

A faction of the time.

Dear Wicked Cousin Turbulence,

The slick heel of your hand has left a print on the glass-topped table.
Please advise. Zorba frets the punctuation. Zorba establishes his case
of fine jewels and silver monies. He repairs his watch chain
at the sideboard. He shoots a look. In the morning,
we will be forced to further.

The progeny gets it. The prim cupboard turns its back and we thirst,
we detail, we dip the pendant like a spoon into the broth, the tumbler
is whole. Your advice will follow? Please advise.

Dear Avon, Dear Lady,

My subtle line wish-washed by Zorba's C-serum, I include the request
for additional funding, equipment, such as the cannon shaped
as a cuticle.

The specter mask on page eleven. The turpentine brassiere.
When in girlhood I encountered the gilt edge of your plethora, Zorba
put her hand to mast. Half-mast. She twisted the miniature dial
and the tube rose, rose to meet my clapboard. Matched.

At the end of the bath, read the bath leaves, the ring and the hollow
skins of the bath beads. Even in the dank, we rinse the strawberry
from our turbans, we frame the jaw with petrol.

Curl it, Zorba. The tin tub waits, the lady, the tramp.

Gets weaker when you treat her like a queen. Gets stuck
in Juárez when it's raining. And it's
Easter time too. Reconciled, she's gonna be up for awhile. Bleeding,
but not so as you'd notice. Tied
to furniture she's never been tied to. Electricity howls in the bones. In her
    brand new
leopard pill box. Dear Black Nordic,
I found it in a plaited hair. Zorba
took the steps by two, requesting
your temperature. Your. Dear Black Arctic,
each letter was doubled and written
for a look in the mirror. Each letter
forged from a tentacle. Each tentacle.
Lashed.

Dear Junior It's Been a Long Time,

Zorba's lights are out behind the ply. If you press your ear
to the slip of gust. If you press your limb from left to right.
The composition reads, records the riptide on your brow.
You would have to stammer. Against my femur.

You will have to stammer against my femur.

Dear classroom, no windows, two slide projectors, humming,

Here is where Zorba recorded my measurements. The chalkboard
rinsed and the numbers frisked. Pinkly. Prickly. Here
the eraser clapped. The clap of thunder. Under the desks,
and Zorba tolled the log truck.

Here is where a ninety-degree angle. A hummingbird knocking.
Too late in the season, I measured the red syrup, I ran the funnel
to the vial, to the window where we seated. In a row. Zorba,
her little nephew, her shotgun, myself. Bubblegum. Bubblegum.

Dear Seamstress,

A wiggle in the eyelid. Zorba pronounced it and I
performed it. Half-hearted. Half-lobed. He noted.
Which fabric bore a renegade variation. The elastic bodice
held tight my premonitions, while, all that while, the hem
crept close and skimmed my knees.

A pin, you maintain. A pin you paint his name on, and, like
a baton, with which he directs.

Dear Doctor Jawbones,

Please administer the Rorschach. Zorba's needing.
Please locate her on your hilarious spectrum. Catch her
baking your cookies near Christmas.
The Christmas tree. On fire. Again. Proverbial.
When you read this like a telegraph stop
you will know stop I made it out stop
alight. Take stop
the metro. Heart the passage and the krylon walls.

Dear Colonel,

In Amherst. In the Dallas Room. Bring a bag up there with you.
Cleaned out, sprayed down. Take a sample from its purveyor
and a complementary yee-haw.

The vote was split. I said aye and Zorba nay. We cannot
expect you. About half as much. The bone should be no shock,
the crew raise no brow, and the terminal degree a full plow.

In summation. A currency of dogs from wolves, of foxes tamed, the Siberian
scientist lonely in his foxglove, leveraged by the farmers. They
run as puppets do. They travel in style. Do tell.

Dear Bioneers,

I see your former California through this pickle jar. The chestnut
of its coastline, Zorba's first lover crowned in its postmark. The zoo
then rife with fruit and wine, the trolley with a whisking of hair
and cellulose glue. I see your California bloodmoss, aphrodisiac, plenty.

What paunches they developed, what circumspect manners. A pinky
in the dishdrain, the telephone in a civilized outfit. The man
himself had an electronic addition. He buzzed in the foyer,
the wrinkle in his chest pocket sang, it was the decaffeinated eye
of the nightingale story. I rang my knife on the edge of the glass.

I asked for water. And water again. And was my bear wound, was my
wince against the bedskirt, was my different illness from yours—

Dear Captain of Industry,

I protected my creature with a complicated rigging. I took twofold
the barb and twofold the batting. Even the sail wore epaulets.
Epoxy. My twin concerns folded neatly, collapsible, into the saucers,
the saucers into the game hens, and the game hens into the oven,
otherwise used for storage. For shortage. I shorted the sheets

of the privates. In this context, Zorba was not so much obsolete
as obscure. I called his name in only the most ordinary sports.

A game of spud. The category so often returned to flowering trees,
so often dogwood came out of my mouth. My acrostic pout.

Dear Curved Drive,

The lubbers commiserate. Wrongheaded, samurai-masked, foot
the sod perimeter. They've taught me newfangled math. Calcs.
They describe the angle at which I angled out of the window,
where they found me. Hung up on the neighbors' lamppost.

A bead cramps every surface. Its engine off. Rolling
specter of a chassis. Gravel gone to talc. Talcs.

Dear Zorba,

Keep your voice down.

Dear Ridge of a Rib in My Ribcage,

Rotate the cord neatly in its socket. The sandpaper retired,
but the powder on the cement belies. From here, you employ
a stethoscope, a valve that is shaped as such and a string
with no center. In other words, not braided. To detangle.

Information. Dote on me, now. Recite the story you heard
Zorba whisper against my swathing. As a smallpox. I wore slippers
that shuttled me out of the incubator, onto the interlocking.

I am meant to measure you with a metal device. Which device
resembles a hole punch. I am meant to trick you onto this scale,
situating a small cake in a checkerboard cloth over the rubber lap.

Dear Tilly, Dear Hermes,

Enclosed, please find Zorba's lamb shank. Please find a coveted booklet.
A prerequisite. In the future, when you shadow, please find a subtle
distinction between street and theater.

I craze the window in her butchered sedan. I leverage her documents,
spilling from the console. Figure these. Repeat.

Dear Pearce & Pearce, Inc.,

I trail your feathered leavings. I see around the ground-level,
cracked half-panes where you've been tramping. A bitty crescent
told off by a length of slit hose, where the leaves molder, and
what you leave molders. A sparkplug.

Tell me, said Zorba, do he & he make you feel for your temperature?
Do he & he have a muscle big in the arm from the aiming? Do he
& he pay for it when you dine at the surgeon's? And I say.

Every time. Here is my wallet, my truncated prescription.
Purse your lips. A regatta of providers ensues.

Dear Premonitions,

I am waiting for your teeth to lose their grip on the rope.
That spins. I examine each of your vivid feathers as they fall
to the sawdust. Your fishnets ring in the strobe.

I have removed each tiny blemish from my back with a palette knife.
Zorba has measured my fluid and determined. Viscosity. Each
revolution frays near the apparatus. Zorba taught me well
how to prepare a gelatin slide. How to exacerbate a crevice.

When your winged tiara, your magnificent profile, your slipper.
I will be still. I will be netless and swift.

Dear Debacler,

I saw your filament slick. I saw you spindle near that gutter.
You split your screen in two. To be one man and another.
You angled two cameras, one at each of your tarantulas. Your back
erupted in chorus. Zorba claimed she had never voted

for you. She claimed when she told me not to vote
for the woman with the cabbage rose lodged in her throat,
and later when. She told me Walter Mondale lived beneath
the compost bin. An oil with a pregnant friend.

Dear Grandmother,

Zorba's winding her bedsheet. In a tunnel, there are two forks.
Two crows with a winch. I'm enclosing the tourniquet. Credulous.

Mimeograph: Frond I

We went to the cakewalk. Musical chairs, spaghetti
peeled hair, peeled grapes. Grappa. Zorba had great
interest in the Siamese twins. He said their dress
would be a two-dress stitched together. He said bone
fuse. He worked in a new pomade.

I imagined the sequined curtain my bed, my shower curtain.
Mechanically I counted teeth with tongue, with rows with
velvety rose seats, and wondered. The doubling. The juncture
at the hip bone, no big thing. Spur and "fuse."

Succession: A Translation

I traveled the meat-paved road. I obtained an afterlife. The girl-scout badge

Studded my pelvic bones with bones. An oar-shaped fragment. Fossil.
& my tongue, a fossil

Before Zorba got to me. Before the Twenty Agonies took it
out of me. Took out my three souls. A string, & pet the other two
into tiny pieces

Dislodged, in tall, baroque wigs, my vermillion-veined organs flicked.
Bugles, reptilian tongues & concrete urns brought inside to dry.

Reclined on the sentimental expanse of pink shag carpet
like Zsa Zsa Gábor on amphetamines, & watched the haints
behind the machines, my Zorba

& No one ever guessed that I died. The same.
With a sash of tears hanging out of one eye. With a chrome heart
hysterical & large as an ox.

In the hamstring, Zorba, I drafted that tightness. My blinds
a twisty gray and the lino clumped and dander. Despite
the fog of wealth in clay. Despite the articulate scavenge.
A proper "red dress."

Burial.

The flare in my arm as an anthill will, and I called you
to drain it. To procure and package the tool of hollowing.
Hallowing. Sheepish.

Mimeograph: Frond II

Zorba sent me a preparatory filling wrapped in white cotton tissue.
The actual tooth. And the fibrous root. It was not an act of *pharmacy,*
or even *pharmakon,* so much as *pharmacide.* In the study garden, a plot
of Manchurian baby's breath gone to seed. The braille became coy
and archaic in equal measure, a punchbox detailing an athletic extinction.

And then I was asked to make the double *l,* which required the turgid
sleigh of my tongue. My test results had been peeled apart before arrival.
My wicked little eggwhites ran the length of transit.

On a Torn Divan

Dear Aunt and Uncle Tourniquet. Zorba's days are numbered.
He wears them around his wrist on a leather watchband. Torn.
The edges swish. He exacerbates the whitened collar.
He purchased shares in a candy store and placed them in name.

His basketball weathers. His team plate.

But Zorba's onto this.

Here, take my brooch, says Zorba. You look like a pitcher
of tap water. You look like a red ribbon run through
a garbage disposal, you wear like an old drape. Take pinch
to your cheek, take pluck and curl, take penicillin in massive

(doses.)

Iron
On

When Zorba prayed for me, I ducked. My trickle
went on for a week. The stewardess said, the airline, it was
all nontransferable. The heart beat. The hearthrug beat
to shreds, my own rug loose and coiled. And my organ
like an iron dervish.

Supposing Zorba's bible fell open, she took its advice. She
took an anemone to her little nephew, blued with a fuzzy eye,
and she bathed him. Note: his lashes clumped.

Note: his ringlets woozy. A talcum paste.

An iron-on. On.

(MIMEOGRAPH: FROND III

Later, locking him in the dog's cage, I would almost acey-deucy, I would
almost arcane arachnid, I would almost ach-ach heist. I would grief with a
handful of cat food, and crunch same into a chocolate pudding. I would beg
him tilt his ankle over, place them, thighs apart and woosh.)

I am up to my lungs in Zorba's timeline. Flecks of charcoal
in the water glass, the bellwether. I have been advised
to position a keen little stone, or a ragged bit of glass, not
so fragile as to shatter, in the toe of my riding boot. Advised
to knot my own toes thusly, to relieve them precisely, to weave
a pattern of discomfort.

If questioned, I would have to say that indeed I soaked the petal
of a large-mouthed bloom against a wound I'd given myself shaving.
Indeed buried it in the southern corner of Zorba's vegetable garden,
near the radishes, the ravishes. Indeed I thought it would produce.
Indoctrinate. I was a year off from menses.

Zorba's nails, in those years, were the grim of gasoline. Her weeds
were hired out, her little yellow cushion curdled beneath the knees
of neighbor girls. The willow trees a dirty pest, a skirt shifting.

The night of May the twenty-ninth. I had a petty ghost in the tubes.
Resid. Zorba's Eve was on point for the occasion. On pink.
And blue pills. With a wound they flushed it out. Or portions.
Wordage. Zorba's Eve displayed a model symmetry, the trinity
of organs, a belt.

A belt to nuzzle the bandage, its silver buckle like a disco
against the skin. The film. Ingmar Bergman.

The delineation was so. Superficial.

(Sweets)

With my face dirtied. With a handful of silver nuggets
perennial. I took Zorba. I took Zorba's watch
to the apothecary. I asked for a dram. A doctor's worth
of malaria. The regulation. Of pills. For a trip.
For a discussion in the cockpit. I'd like to go south.
I'd like an ice with that. To ice you.

(Sweets)

Zorba asked me to deliver this speech. A birthing.
A tweezer and an antigen. Insecticide. I took extra care
in applying my makeup, affixing an eyelash, deleting
a red herr. My eyes were ruddy with grief. I said
to the inspector. Excuse me. I have not made
the coffee. I haven't a coffee spoon, marmalade,
a clue. As to what. I didn't mean to sound as such,
but to hedge. I took some sugar from its milken spot.

Acknowledgments

Warm thanks to those publications in which some of these missives first appeared:

"A Quarter-Hour of Recess" in *American Letters & Commentary;* "Actuary,""Beneficial,""A Parsimonious Holiday," and "A Second Opinion Is Sought" in *Apocryphal Text;* "Tribune" in *Bird Dog;* "Fondly, Yours, Sincerely, My Love,""My Sea Legs,""Rallying on the Plank, the Porch Swing Leans In," and "(Sweets)" in *Chicago Review;* "Building a Nest, the A–Z," "Nailed into the Mantel, the Wool Unravels [here untitled],""The Pinned-up Nurse [here untitled]," and "Tangled in the Linens, the Cold Sweat [here untitled]" in *Coconut Poetry;* "Dear classroom, no windows, two slide projectors, humming,""Née Providential,""The Unhomely Kinder [here untitled],""Wading Through the Hope Chest, a Bleater [here untitled]," and "What Historicity" in *Conjunctions;* "A Transportation Ballad" in *Court Green;* "Dear Aunt Hemorrhage, Dear Uncle Rottweiler," "Dear Grandma," "Dear Martin Grainger,""Dear Ridge of a Rib in My Ribcage" in *Dead Horse Review;* "Dear Captain of Industry," Dear Colonel""Dear Pearce & Pearce, Inc." in *Denver Quarterly;* "Dear Avon, Dear Lady,""Dear Argyle Our Frosty Morning,""Dear Curved Drived," "Dear Premonitions" in *mem;* "Mimeograph: Frond I," "Mimeograph: Frond II," and "(Mimeograph: Frond III" in *Parakeet;* and "The Hung Over Gibbous [here untitled],""Iron On,""Were the Drawing Room a Portion" in *Salt Hill.*

"Dear Pearce & Pearce, Inc.," appeared in *Best American Poetry 2007,* edited by Heather McHugh.

"Succession: A Translation" rips/riffs off Lara Glenum's "How to Obtain the Girl Scout Badge for Succeeding in the Afterlife," from *Hounds of No* (Action Press, 2005).

Page 24 spins out of a scene from the film *The Lady Eve* (1941).

Page 26 contains a found language translation from the Mapuche language Mapudungun.

Page 28 contains found language.

Additional warm gratitude extended to the following actors, who may or may not be aware of their agency: Shanna Compton, Lara Glenum, Johannes Göransson, Heidi Lynn Staples, Claudia Rankine, Dr. Jed Rasula, Dr. Caroline Desbiens, Dr. Bonnie Dow, Emily Shelton, the Washington County Fair, David Trinidad, *Mad Shadows* (Marie-Claire Blais), *Middlesex* (Jeffrey Eugenides), *Mommy Dearest, Taking Charge of Your Fertility* (Toni Weschler), *Motherhood Lost: A Feminist Account of Pregnancy Loss in America* (Linda Layne), Ziggy Stardust, Kristin Hersh ("Gets weaker when you treat [her] like a queen," p. 45), Bob Dylan ("in Juárez when it's raining. And it's / Easter time too," "Electricity howls in the bones. In her / brand new leopard pillbox hat," p. 45), Paul Simon ("Reconciled, [she's] gonna be up for awhile," p. 45), Tom Waits ("Bleeding, / but not so as you'd notice," p. 45), and Temple House in County Sligo.

Thank you Adam, thank you Hazel.

Danielle Pafunda is the author of *Pretty Young Thing* (Soft Skull Press, 2005), and the chapbook *A Primer for Cyborgs: The Corpse* (Whole Coconut Chapbook Series, forthcoming). Her poems have been chosen three times for *Best American Poetry* (2004, 2006, and 2007). Other poems and reviews have appeared in such publications as *American Letters & Commentary*, *Conjunctions*, the *Georgia Review*, and *TriQuarterly*. She is coeditor of the online journal *La Petite Zine*, a doctoral candidate in the University of Georgia's creative writing program, and Spring 2008 Poet-in-Residence at Columbia College Chicago.

Printed in the United States
123336LV00011BA/256/P

9 780615 195933